POSTERS *OF THE NINETEEN-TWENTIES*

POSTERS

OF THE NINETEEN-TWENTIES

Maurice Rickards

WALKER AND COMPANY, NEW YORK

First published in the United States of America in 1968 by Walker and Company, a division of the Walker Publishing Company, Inc.

Published simultaneously in Canada by The Ryerson Press, Toronto.

Library of Congress Catalog Card Number: 68–22131.

Printed and bound in Great Britain.

List of Illustrations

The Nineteen-twenties

Shimmering in the glow of retrospect, the 1920s have become a legend before they are quite dead. As we push into the 'seventies the mechanisms of nostalgia work overtime; for fear of looking forward, we look back. After all, we have to look somewhere. Those who are older gaze back over the heads of the young ones to a dimly recollected world; it is a world that youth has pieced together from its debris—to make something that is new and strange to both. What were they really like, the 1920s? Before the psychedelic haze comes down for good, let us take a last look.

There was plenty to look at. There was Lindbergh's flight from New York to Paris; there was the first demonstration of television; there was Marie Stopes with her lectures at Queen's Hall; there was the founding of the Union of Soviet Socialist Republics. *Winnie the Pooh* came out. So did *Mein Kampf.*

The decade got off to a big start. 1920 was hardly a fortnight old when America's Eighteenth Amendment to the Constitution came into force. Under it the manufacture, sale or transportation of intoxicating liquors 'for beverage purposes' was prohibited. Somebody called it 'the greatest social experiment of modern times'. It was to last for thirteen years. In the year that it started, one J. T. Thompson invented the sub-machine gun, which was to play a notable part in it.

In the same year H. G. Wells, 55-year-old survival from another century, published his *Outline of History. Time and Tide* appeared for the first time, Mary Pickford married Douglas Fairbanks, and at a place called Writtle the first public broadcasting service in the world, directed by G. Marconi, started transmissions. The Empress Eugenie, widow of Napoleon III, died. The League of Nations came into existence. At an art exhibition in Cologne, visitors were invited to smash up the exhibits, which they did.

There was a lot more to come. Faced with the stupefying total of over 30 million men killed or wounded in the war, the world seemed set on guaranteeing that nothing would ever be the same again. In Germany the National Socialist party had just been formed; within six weeks Italy had seen the founding of the *Fasci del Combattimento*. In Britain, Rutherford and Chadwick were launched on the series of experiments that were to lead to the splitting of the atom; they had already disintegrated most of the elements. In the United States the Ku-Klux-Klan showed up again—bigger. In Britain the Austin Seven arrived. In Paris, James Joyce wrote *Ulysses*. The cocktail was invented. *Time* magazine appeared. Peter Sellers was born. With Al Jolson in *The Jazz Singer*, sound films came in.

Fleming discovered penicillin; Geiger invented his counter. India came up with Ghandi, Italy with Mussolini, and Germany with Hitler. D. H. Lawrence came up with *Lady Chatterley*.

British women got the vote. Wall Street crashed. The expression 'apartheid' first appeared. Salvador Dali first appeared. The photo-flash bulb was introduced; so was Perspex. The planet Pluto was discovered. Warner Brothers announced that they would never make another black-and-white film.

Toward the end of the period there was a harvest of war-recall: *All Quiet on the Western Front, Journey's End, Hell's Angels* appeared within months of each other. A pope (Pius XI) left the Vatican for the first time. The *Graf Zeppelin* flew round the world. Byrd flew over the South Pole. Amy Johnson flew solo from London to Australia. It was all go.

The four years of the Great War had brought death and disaster to millions. But to other millions it had brought liberation. For the fighting of the war the world had mobilised a total of a hundred million men; to do the jobs they left behind them a hundred million women moved in. This was no emancipation; it was a conceded takeover. Under cover of the larger battle, without so much as a chain or a railing, the battle for women's rights was won. Heavily

DET
MUNTRE
HJÖRNE
FESTARRAN=
GEMENT
MED
DANS
BÖGELUND · 1920
TIVOLI

camouflaged, there had been a social revolution. Short skirts, short hair; Marie Stopes and Black-Bottom . . They would be smoking next. . .

In less than a decade the whole structure of family life had changed. The New Woman had arrived. In times gone by there had been repeated waves of New Women; Nightingale started one, so did Marie Curie, so did Amelia Bloomer. But this really was a new woman—universal and for keeps. She even had a permanent wave.

In a parallel breakthrough a big new industry emerged; travel and entertainment—only yesterday the pleasure of the gentry—was now a game that everyone could play. Dancing, the wireless, jazz, talking pictures—these were new and universal stimulants. So was the thrill of moving around; the motor car and the aeroplane made light of distance; life acquired new dimensions.

These were stimulants with a double role: they held promise for the future, and they helped to cloud the memory, not only of the immediate past, but of the world that had led up to it. It was goodbye to a world now pathetically irrelevant, a world unmasked as a phoney. With gathering intensity, a mood grew up. It found expression in all media and in most countries. Even the places that had escaped the direct impact of the war fell in with it; it was the mood of emancipation.

To the fidgety tempo of the new music, with cigarette-holder, low-slung waist, silk stockings and twirling beads, the new woman attended the launching of the new age. Suddenly, as though by common consent, everything began to look different; the sights and sounds of everyday life broke out in a new pattern. Posters—as usual—were among the first to break.

The Tivoli poster typifies the trend—both in style and content. Copenhagen's pleasure garden, long famous as an evening playground, now stepped up its pleasures to the faster, louder, jazzier beat. The poster says it all. With its nervous angularity, the abandon of its figures, the twitch and jerk of its airborne wording, the design expresses the explosive restlessness of a society suddenly

Tivoli Gardens, Copenhagen 1920 (Denmark) *Bögelund*

made free. Not least of its symptoms is the contrived breach of the poster's boundaries, a footloose breakthrough into unrespectability. The new world—even for the neutrals—was here at last.

It was a world of miles per hour. The motor car was everywhere. By 1924 the total number of motor vehicles in Britain alone was over half a million. That meant one motor car to every 74 people. (The figure for the 'sixties is 1 to 7.) Only twenty years before, the first motor race had yielded an. average speed of 15 mph. At Daytona Beach in 1927 Major Seagrave clocked up just over 203 mph. It was in the 'twenties that the fast car began to acquire the status image that was to stay with it into the 'sixties and 'seventies. (Lazza's poster for the Milan Circuit event is an accurate preview—almost fifty years before its time—of the wheel-level shots in Cinerama's *Grand Prix*, made in the late 'sixties.)

Even more spectacular were the goings-on in the air. In 1925 (the year of *Mein Kampf*) the Schneider Cup was won at an *average* speed of 232 mph. In a balloon race from Belgium, the winner came down in Brittany, over 400 miles away, and the airship R33 managed to get safely back from an unscheduled trip over the North Sea and the Dutch coast after being torn from her mooring mast in a storm. At Farnborough, Captain Courtney made a successful vertical ascent and descent in a 'windmill plane'. Regular passenger air services had been inaugurated between London and Paris, and there was air mail (discontinued during the winter months) from London to most of Northern Europe. You could post a letter in London at 10 o'clock in the morning and it would reach Paris that same evening. (How about that?) Over longer distances there was a plane-train-ship-train system, not quite so fast; but on alternate Thursdays you could post a letter in London at 6 o'clock in the evening and it would be in Baghdad only nine days later—a saving of up to nine days on the ordinary post.

Communications were getting better all the time. As well as cable links, the GPO had wireless contact with nearly a dozen

Circuito di Milano (Monza Race Track). 1923 (Italy) *Lazza*

CIRCVITO DI MILANO

NEL PARCO REALE DI MONZA · 3·10 SETTEMBRE 1922
GRAN PREMIO DELL'A.C.D'ITALIA · 500.000 LIRE DI PREMI
NAZIONI ISCRITTE: ITALIA · FRANCIA · INGHILTERRA · GERMANIA · AVSTRIA

countries; the new super-power radio station at Rugby—with an aerial $1\frac{1}{2}$ miles long—brought Britain into touch with the whole world.

As well as bringing people into touch with the outside world, radio was bringing people into touch with themselves; the 'twenties saw the rise of a huge new community—the great Company of Listeners. For the first time it became possible to speak to everybody all at once; for the first time a man could know the news as soon as the papers did—sooner, if he was smart and could listen to some of the foreigners. From a million backyards, there sprouted aerials.

There was another thing: in addition to the headphones—only a step down the street there were The Pictures. With the coming of the 'twenties there flickered into being a habit that for many was to become a lifelong addiction. The seed of the Edison Company's Life-Size Animated Pictures had given fruit.

Into the lives of ordinary people everywhere came new names: René Claire, Hitchcock, Eisenstein, Cecil B. de Mille, Goldwyn. Further in came names like Garbo, Chaplin, Veidt, Novarro, Dietrich, Pickford and Mickey Mouse. Within a decade there was brought into existence a whole new mythology. Valentino, already immortal by 1925, was dead by 1926. As polyglot as its cast lists, the industry was to establish a world idiom; it became one of the major formative influences of post-war society. It was not long before the Hays Office and the British Board of Film Censors emerged—brought into being by the industry itself in its own defence.

Nobody censored the industry's posters. For the most part these were letterpress renderings of the film title and its cast, locally printed on a standard cinema contents bill. Only occasionally did we see a designed job like the one for *l'Amant Eternel*—celluloid's answer to the *Moulin Rouge* and *Toulouse Lautrec*. Here is the authentic leg- and midriff-exposure of early Hollywood; here is

Astra Paris Films (Rudolph Valentino in *The Eternal Lover*), 1926 (France)
Anonymous

12

Rudolph
Valentino

dans

ASTRA
PARIS
FILMS

L'AMANT ETERNEL
(LE FILS DU CHEIK)

IMP. BEDOS PARIS

the full flower of the Valentino sex image. At his lying-in-state, which took place in the year the poster appeared, there was a queue eleven blocks long.

Kodak's answer to Toulouse-Lautrec was different. It was yet another of life's new excitements: *still* pictures, that you took yourself. The Shepperson drawing of the girl in the striped dress is everything that the 'twenties ought to have been—and, to some people, undoubtedly were. Here is the idyllicism of *Now We Are Six* (not A. E. Sheppard, but coincidentally close) with the prettiness and airiness of a children's middle-class world—a world as yet untouched by Rutherford and Chadwick, *Ulysses* and the Ku-Klux-Klan. But it is a far cry too, from the seaside world of yesterday's 1890s, when the six-inch leg of the swimsuit would have been quite indecently brief.

But for all the sweetness and light—whether at the Tivoli Gardens or Frinton-on-Sea, there were undertones that no-one could ignore.

In Britain the homes fit for heroes to live in had by no means all materialised. Against a background of emancipation and tenor saxophones, there was growing awareness of poverty and unemployment. The British National Debt (raised almost entirely for the purpose of fighting wars), and standing modestly in 1914 at some £650 million, had risen by 1920 to nearly £8,000 million. In June 1921, the official unemployment figure was 2,580,429. In the following years it settled down to around the $1\frac{1}{2}$ million mark. Falling profits, particularly in the privately-owned coal-mines, brought threats of even lower wages. These in turn brought strikes. In the first five years of the 'twenties Britain lost 150 million working days through strikes. For the twelve months of 1926, year of the General Strike, the figure was 160 million. For nine days in the May of that year, as *Ben Hur* thundered out over the dog-ends and peanut-shells, there was silence almost everywhere. Silence on the railways, in road transport, in the iron and steel industries,

Kodak c. 1923 (Britain) *Claude Shepperson*

14

Take a Kodak with you.

in building and in printing. There were armoured cars in the streets of London.

The gaiety and gloss of the nightclub 'twenties had only limited validity. In the heart of Empire a ventricle was wheezing. Throughout the world there were rumblings of an economic evolution; in Brazil the economy collapsed under a mountainous heap of unprofitable coffee; in the USSR they started a 5-Year Plan; in America things were building up to the crash of the Stock Exchange and the world convulsion of the 'thirties. For the man in the street there was not much by way of solid comfort. Too often he was uncomfortably close to the pavement's edge.

Like everyone else, the poster put a brave enough face on it. With its jazz and jitter, with its assertive restlessness, it made an unmistakable break with practically everything. But there was more to the break than just the nervous angularity of the Tivoli Gardens. There was another element—one that dated back through the haze to the 1890s—the element of extreme simplicity. Toulouse-Lautrec had started it, and through all the shot and shell and social revolution, it had never petered out.

The style of Sven Brasch's *Casino* poster, with its audacious neglect of all but the minimum, its commanding use of basics—this captures the re-birth of a movement that was to sweep everything before it. It was to find its full expression in Cassandre, in E. McKnight Kauffer, and ultimately in Henrion and Abram Games.

Back in 1913 there had been a free and easy flow of design exchange—the ordinary interpenetration of ideas that crystallises into universal trends. Overspilling national frontiers, the great poster names, the Steinlens, the Muchas, Beggarstaffs, Beardsleys, Bradleys and Penfields had coalesced. There had been different threads of style, different accents, different personalities, but over all there emerged a discernible direction. With the war, this cross-fertilisation stopped. Cut off from each other, designers pursued

Casino 1925 (Denmark) *Sven Brasch*

16

CASINO

L. 8

TELF. 1951

SYNDERINDEN

their own ways. All over Europe—all over the world, in fact—war posters had developed independent idioms. In 1918 the lights had gone up again and there was a general scurry round to see what the other fellow had been doing. To everybody's surprise the directions had remained much the same; the immediate upshot was Tivoli Garden nineteentwentyitis, the side-effect was the simplicity of Brasch.

As always, there were the old standbys, the traditional 'fine art' posters. These broke no new ground at all. The Pears' Soap 'Bubbles' boy of the 1890s had its counterpart in the Bisto kids, and Cappiello's 1923 design for the opening of the Théâtre de l'Etoile was only the trot of a hansom cab from 1900. And as always there were the oddities that turned up because the managing director happened to know an artist chap.

But the big new common denominator was simplicity. If in Lautrec's day it had been true that the poster was a simple statement for the eye of the busy passer-by, how abundantly true was it now. With mounting chaos in the streets and the tempo of everything multiplied by at least two, it was clear that only the simplest of messages could get through.

Added to that there was a bright new public, quick on the uptake, more given to brevity, more open to visual signals, increasingly literate. (It was the period when the word *sophistication* came in.) Just as the jokes in *Punch* had dropped their dialogues and stage directions, just as the curlicues and visual trimmings of Victoriana had gone, so it was with the flurry of pre-war poster detail. Kitchener, with his pointing finger and *Your Country Needs You* had introduced an urgency and directness that went well with the world of fast cars and Rugby Radio.

The bold, dynamic visual statement came into its own. The designer's problem was twofold. There was the battle with the

Théâtre de l'Etoile 1923 (France) *Cappiello*

18

THÉÂTRE DE L'ÉTOILE
PROCHAINEMENT
OUVERTURE DU
THÉÂTRE DE L'ÉTOILE
136 CHAMPS ÉLYSÉES.
AVEC UNE
COMÉDIE NOUVELLE
DE
SACHA GUITRY
JOUÉE PAR
SACHA GUITRY
ET
YVONNE
PRINTEMPS
ATELIER D'ART DEVAMBEZ
1923

client before the job was begun. This was the battle to bring him into line with Kitchener—to get rid of as many unnecessary ingredients as possible and to simplify the basic message. Then there was the battle with the design itself, a reduction of the finally-agreed message to the simplest visual terms. But simplicity on its own was not enough. It had to be simple and striking, or simple and attractive, or simple and intriguing, or simple and persuasive—or simple and funny.

Simple and funny was often easiest. Particularly in Britain where visual tricks are less readily grasped than verbal ones, there was a tendency to opt for humour—and to tie the humour to a turn of words. Many of Britain's most memorable posters have been in this category. Hassall's joke for Andrews, familiar to two or three generations, raises the same sort of smile that the Skegness bounding fisherman still gets. (He, by Hassall too, has lasted half a century.) These posters seek no more than to be agreeable; they are of the same genre as the 'hunting' Bisto kids—*Ready for the Meat*—(page 63), Bovril's immortal *Prevents that Sinking Feeling* —(page 35) and the Pears' Soap tramp of the 1890s with his *I used your soap two years ago. Since then I have used no other.* These, while they fulfil the requirement of simplicity—and certainly of memorability—do so on a purely verbal basis. Without their captions their humour, and their impact, would be much diminished.

To say that they seek no more than to be agreeable is to beg a question. The psychology of the poster has always been—and still is—an uncertain science. It may well be that in being agreeable they sell more liver salts and Skegness than other gambits ever would. Their effectiveness, like that of all advertising, now or in the 'twenties, is difficult to measure. Said one advertiser 'I know that half of what I spend on advertising is wasted, but I don't know which half.'

It is in the late 'sixties, with increasing expenditure on TV

Andrews Liver Salt 1925 (Britain) *John Hassall*

20

advertising, that the true poster begins to make its exit. It is destined, if it survives at all, to do so only as a supporting sideshow to the television circus. But from our vantage point at the end of the poster line we see at last the cumulative goodwill that these simple jokes acquired. There is more than just nostalgia in the smiles that they can still raise today.

Perhaps no item of human paraphernalia has been so exhaustively presented in advertising as the bottle—particularly in posters, and particularly the bottle alcoholical. Prior to the arrival of the Barclay's Lager poster it had been insisted that the bottle be shown in as full and detailed a glory as possible. What else, after all, was there to show? With great daring, Barclays broke the rules. Designed by an unnamed hero in a London advertising agency, the poster comes firmly into the category of simple and intriguing. It has the distinction—as rare in the 'twenties as it is today—of presenting its subject by implication rather than by laboriously detailed statement. As a study in economy it is exemplary; as an evocation of refreshment it is superb. In its unorthodox reversal of tones, in its coolness and clarity, it says a great deal about Barclay's London Lager.

Simplicity of this order is a direct descendant of the Beggarstaffs. Thirty years before, in as intensive a burst of poster virtuosity as the world had seen, James Pryde and William Nicholson had launched themselves as the first double-act—the Beggarstaff Brothers. In the two years that they collaborated they produced posters of revolutionary simplicity. Their work was to bring a new meaning to the word 'poster'—a meaning that it has managed to retain to this day. Their poster for Henry Irving's production of *Don Quixote* is still a landmark in the history of the graphic arts. It was also,

Barclay's London Lager 1925 (Britain) *Anonymous*

BARCLAY'S
LONDON
LAGER

unfortunately for everybody concerned, a quarter of a century before its time.

Its time was really now, in the 1920s—perhaps even now in the 'sixty/'seventies.

In its modest way the Barclay's poster, like the Danish *Casino* design, was a picking-up of threads. It was a return to Pryde and Nicholson.

But the battle for simplicity was a hard one. In Britain there was still something faintly disturbing in the simple poster. Kitchener had pointed the way, it is true, but there were limits. To eyes accustomed to the simplicities of Andrews and the Bisto kids (and still not quite unmindful of 'Bubbles') the Barclay's Lager look was simplicity that bordered on severity. Could we not have simplicity with *feeling*? Did it necessarily have to be stark, to be 'modern'?

There was a spate of compromise. With treatments only once removed from the nursery and the greeting card—and with rigid adherence to the rules of modernity—designers began to serve up simplicity in softer mood. There emerged a mixture of Kodak idyllic and Beggarstaff impact. It was a kick in the pants with a velvet boot—and it was not without a certain charm. Frank Gayton's poster for Somnus Bedding is typical; with its rejection of the brutality of the Barclay's Lager treatment, and yet with its obvious concession to the basic idiom, it expresses the predicament of its time. It is design, as you might say, at the awkward age. The Somnus treatment just gets away with it, but it cannot be denied that there were also terrible excesses.

The compromise that the Gayton style embodies is British. It was part of the compromise that there had to be all the way round. It was not only in design that trends seemed incompatible. It ran throughout everything. There was the incompatibility of the generations; of cocktails and the Cenotaph; of unemployment and the Charleston. There was the new Fascist Italian government; and almost simultaneously there was this new thing called the Union of Soviet Socialist Republics. Nothing seemed to match up with

Somnus Bedding 1925 (Britain) *Frank Gayton*

SOMNUS BEDDING
'GOOD NIGHT'

anything. The old order stuck to its guns—and to its stuffed shirts; for the new order, anything went; for the out-of-works there was little to stick to and little to do. For all of them the cost of peace was going up and up.

Before the war you could have had an eight-course dinner at Lyons Popular for two and six (eleven courses if you went to another shilling). Today dining out was expensive. Prices had almost doubled. The standard rate of income tax—one and twopence in the pound in 1914—had risen by leaps and bounds. By the end of the war it had reached five shillings in the pound. It went even higher. In 1919 and 1920 it was six shillings. Even now, with everything allegedly back to normal, it was four and sixpence. If you had an income of over £4,000 a year there was a new thing called super tax—an extra ninepence in the pound over the ordinary rate. Things were by no means good.

Frank Newbould's diner-out (simplified *à la mode*) is a sign of the times. Even if they did throw in an orchestra and a vocalist, six shillings and seven-and-six was a lot of money for a meal. But the poster's real significance lies in its reliance—in the middle of a social revolution—on the snob appeal of the monocle and the old-time trappings of affluence. With masterly economy Newbould conveys not only information but the very essence of an atmosphere. Here is the leisured world of the *bon viveur*; the peace and prosperity and the stable social order that the war had been fought and won for.

We must allow the possibility that this anonymous restaurant was in fact a cut *below* the Newbould level. Perhaps the image was aspiration rather than fact. But the poster's invocation of the upper crust suggests that the social revolution had still some way to go. However far it had gone, and whatever the truth about the Newbould Index, we observe from the pasted-over price strip that the cost of it all was going up. Where would it end?

It had been in the heart of London (perhaps only around the corner from this very restaurant) that a political exile from Germany

Dinner 1924 (Britain) *Frank Newbould*

NEWBOULD

DINNER
6/- & 7/6 & à la carte
ORCHESTRA & VOCALIST

had sat in a Dean Street attic writing a book. But that was some sixty years before; when he had died and been buried in Highgate cemetery, London had soon forgotten both him and his book. The book was *Das Kapital.*

When on the night of July 16th, 1918 Citizen and Citizeness Romanov, late of the Imperial Palace, were shot in a house in Ekaterinburg—London remembered. Two days later the big Allied counter-attack opened up across the Marne; for a while Russia went out of focus again.

As the universal smoke began to lift it was seen that not only in Europe had there been changes.

It is in the 'sixties that posters of the revolution period have fully emerged to the world at large; they show a drive and vigour often far in advance of their contemporaries. Russia's posters during the early years of the war had had the orthodox look of old Imperial Russia. It was the reluctant turn-of-the-century look. Heavily weighted in favour of the 1870s, they featured declamatory soldiers, double-headed Imperial eagles and sobering calls for subscriptions to a $5\frac{1}{2}$ per-cent War Loan. With the revolution the style changed together with the content. In a dramatic leap into the middle of the twentieth century, Russian graphic design kicked over the imperial traces.

There is a familiar air about the admonishing old gentleman in the Co-operative poster. It is from behind an outsize *YOU* that this latter-day Kitchener jabs a finger and it is in classic mood of individual command that he calls us, not this time into the army, but into the *ko-operativa.* (If his tone is noticeably more urgent we must put it down to difference of temperament, but we speculate as to whether it was by accident or design that the ingredients of this appeal are identical with those of Alfred Leete's Kitchener poster.) Like the Kitchener design, this one in its context also makes a break with tradition. In strength, simplicity and dramatic

YOU—not yet a member of the co-operative—JOIN NOW c. 1923 (USSR)
Anonymous

ЕЩЕ НЕ ЧЛЕН
КООПЕРАТИВА,
— ЗАПИШИСЬ
НЕМЕДЛЕННО!

ЦЕНТРОСОЮЗА

impact it is a graphic treatment that would not be ill at ease in our own time.

For posters, the Russian 1920s were vintage years. But it was to be a long time before we knew.

Meanwhile, back at Margate, Cliftonville, Eastbourne and branches everywhere, the demand for Bobby and Company's evening wraps continued. In a world so recently insecure, with even now the offstage sounds of trouble filtering through, there was something doubly assuring in the old assurance of an evening wrap.

The Bobby poster, ladies' version of the Newbould theme, evoked a wishworld of never-never elegance—an escape hatch from trade depressions, insurrection and rising income tax. Here was an endless summer evening, with Biarritz (or is that Bourne-mouth?) shimmering across the bay. With its up-to-date simplicity, its un-architectural architecture, the sly contrivance of its crescent moon, and the dedicated resolution of its personnel, the setpiece has a sad finality. These times (even if they had ever existed) were never to come again.

The doomy ladies of Margate and Cliftonville are part of the forgotten cargo of the 1920s. Clinging to their inheritance of respectability, committed to a way of life that was ever more irrelevant, their only valid role was as survivors. Their retrospective world was in its way as phoney as the image of the bright young things; like the great new world that was to come, it was becoming increasingly unconvincing.

Forty years later, when the 1920s were to be resurrected as a fashion quirk, the ladies of Margate and Cliftonville remained, like figures on a Greek urn, where they had been left.

It was often to be forgotten how strictly selective an affair the resurrection was. It was only a fractional part of the 'twenties that came back. The short skirts and beads, the waisted lounge suits and the coloured shirts—the whole syndrome of abandon and

Bobby and Company Ltd 1926 (Britain)*Anonymous*

revolt returned, but huge hunks of ordinary 'twenties—the realities
—got left out. So, for the most part, did the Kodak girl and the
Andrews man. So did the Bovril man and the Bisto kids. (So,
certainly, did the Hunger Marches and the General Strike.)

As the age of respectability sank away, the traffic age came in.
The motor car, hardly more than a novelty before the war, had
become an essential nuisance. In unhappy co-existence, horse
and power jostled for position. Soon it was to be just horsepower.
Congestion increased. Traffic accidents went up. A Royal Com-
mission on London's traffic in 1905 had looked into the possibility
of 'better provisions for the organisation and regulation of vehicular
and pedestrian traffic'. Among their findings had been the con-
clusion that traffic volume was increasing to an alarming extent,
that many of the city's roads were too narrow and too cluttered
with obstructions, and that van drivers were inclined to add to the
congestion by foddering their horses at the kerbside. They recom-
mended studies of the possibilities of widening roads, the control
of kerbside standing and the development of overhead rapid
transit systems.

By the 1920s, only twenty years later—nothing had been done.
Soaring from a fatality figure of only one in 1890, by 1919 the
number killed and injured on Britain's roads reached 50,000. By
the end of the 'twenties the figure was 150,000. The City Life
Assurance Company's picture of congestion and danger was only
slightly overdrawn. We observe the postwar detail of the jay-
walkers, the army officer, the sailor, the postman with his shako
hat; the improbable city nursemaid, the topless buses, the
homburgs and the spats. We see that life has moved on a bit.

The genesis of posters is by no means a standardised procedure.
Over the years it has taken many forms. There have been inspired

City Life Assurance 1924 (Britain) *Anonymous*

32

CITY ✦ LIFE

ASSURANCE COMPANY LTD.

Head Office: 36-37, Old Jewry, London, E.C.2.

Claims Paid Exceed £1,600,000.

Assets Exceed
£1,000,000.

Managing Director:
LEONARD ALDRIDGE

adaptations, in which an image first devised for some other purpose altogether is turned into a poster by the simple addition of wording to taste. There have been lucky accidents, where the first random jotting of a designer has found immortality through photo-enlargement. There are the cases where a company had an idea for a poster and got an artist to 'draw it out properly'. Or a member of the public came up with an idea. Or perhaps nobody had any ideas at all, and they called in a poster designer to think of one. The permutations are endless.

Many a poster in advertising's exuberant early years was the outcome of an unsolicited sketch sent in on a postcard. The public at large has always been secretly tickled with the business of advertising; they are delighted to be in on the act. A vicar's daughter, a retired colonel perhaps—somebody would get an idea and jot it down. Of the many such, no poster story has had so odd and unpropitious a beginning as that of *H. H. Harris*. It was to turn out to be one of the good old good ones—a national institution for decades to come.

On the morning of August 16th, 1912, a young schoolboy read in the papers about the sinking of the *Titanic*. It was the greatest maritime disaster in history. Too young to be touched by the full measure of its tragedy, but much impressed with the excitement of it all, he allowed his imagination to dwell upon it. The result was a schoolboy kitchen-table sketch; it showed a pyjamaed man riding happily over the waves on a Bovril jar. Underneath he wrote the words that everybody knows. He sent it off to Bovril.

The Bovril people, with Benson's, their advertising agents, were shocked at the reference, but amused in spite of themselves. It was of course out of the question to use the idea. They filed it away with the other oddments that people had sent in.

Ten years later, going through the file, somebody came on the schoolboy sketch again. It was still rather amusing. With earlier

Bovril 1923 (Britain) *H. H. Harris*

objections now mercifully faded, it was decided to give it a go. But who would do the finished drawing—the professional version to send to the platemaker? They looked about for a reliable professional. In the years that had passed since his kitchen-table days the schoolboy had become a young man. He had also become an artist. As it turned out, with a gap of something over a decade between the original sketch and the final drawing, it was he, young Harris, who rounded off the job.

Another likely young lad at about this time was one E. McKnight Kauffer. He emerges from the poster history of the early 'twenties as a shining—and very soon a guiding—light. His early posters give little indication of the brilliance to come. A poster for the *Daily Herald* in 1918, among the first of his surviving early ones, is untypical of the way he was to develop. So—apart from its uncompromising simplicity—is the Derry and Toms design. Here we see the influence of his elders—a dash of Herrick and a touch of the Newbould (and a curiously bankrupt feature, the pointless double line that sprouts from the word *sale*). But this was the last derivative or pointless thing that Kauffer ever did. And for their role in the shaping of the Kauffer to come, God bless Derry and Toms. (In the early 'twenties the big Kensington stores commissioned work from a number of names that were to become famous—not all of them necessarily as poster artists. Pontings' archives disclose at least two contributions signed *Terence Prentis*—a name to be joined in the years to come by Colman and Varley.)

Kauffer's debut was in a world already well-populated with poster greats: in Britain F. C. Herrick, Aubrey Hammond, Tom Purvis, Austin Cooper, Horace Taylor, Gregory Brown, Frank Newbould; in France, Loupot, Becan, Cassandre and Carlu. There was no designer-shortage. But within three or four years Kauffer was a challenge to them all. Perhaps only Cassandre was to survive

Derry and Toms (publ. 1920) (Britain) *E. McKnight Kauffer*

WINTER SALE

at DERRY & TOMS
KENSINGTON W. 8

comparison. Kauffer was viewed in Britain with admiration bordering on suspicion. ('There is nothing popular in the ordinary sense about Mr Kauffer's work. It is abstract and "advanced". Yet public interest has been aroused to a great degree . . . He is not . . . specifically English in quality.') Kauffer was not at all English. He had in fact arrived as a young man from America. But as a designer he was not American either. When at the end of a long career in Britain he returned to America, his work was regarded as 'British'.

On the continent of Europe he was welcomed as a recognisably new turn in the affairs of the poster. It was to be in the 'thirties, particularly in his work for Frank Pick's London Transport promotion, that he was to find full stature. From the *Daily Herald* and Derry and Toms, in a dozen or so years, he became a world figure.

His Fire of London poster for the London Museum, published in 1922, was a major success. It was a major success again in 1966, when it was republished to mark the 300th anniversary of the fire. Kauffer was not a 'twenties man; of the jazz image and visual boop-a-doop he was no part whatever; he brought to the poster a personal touch—a touch that is universal, timeless and non-pop.

In Britain the 'twenties brought forth as odd a *mélange* of design trends as decades usually do. By the time it had settled down there were roughly four distinguishable schools: there was the department of new-style-turn-of-the-century Hassall *(I must have left it behind)*; there was Newbould Simplified; there was 'modernistic' (Barclays London Mixture)—and there was a style that had at the time no name, but which has since been given one: The Twenties.

The Twenties had specific but indefinable ingredients. They were ingredients that forty years later were to be fastened on as a showbiz/pop-art/fashion fad. The dolly faces and the shoestrap shoes, the sly-innocent look, the candy lettering with the inlaid wiggles—these are the stock-in-trade of the special segment of

London Museum 1922 (Britain) *E. McKnight Kauffer*

LONDON HISTORY AT THE

LONDON MUSEUM

DOVER STREET
OR ST. JAMES'S PARK STATION

the 'twenties that we call The Twenties. In his cabaret poster for Evie de Ropp, Aubrey Hammond sums it up.

Two years on from the boisterous Tivoli Gardens, here The Twenties find their feet. Boisterousness gives way to a certain calm and a sugary insincerity. Less obviously sinister, it has at the same time more than a hint of Beardsley—the other Aubrey, dead this quarter of a century, and in the race memory perhaps never quite forgotten. Like Beardsley it flies in the face of reality; with an obsessive tongue in the cheek it pursues a special make-believe. It creates a fantasy world—not, like the dream of the ladies of Cliftonville, a world of sad nostalgia, but of perverseness. It is manifestly a conceit—contrived, conscious and unashamed. But between the Aubrey of the 'twenties and the other Aubrey there is. only the slenderest similarity. Aubrey Hammond had none at all of the master's dedicated nastiness; if there is something odd about Evie—and about The Twenties image at large—it is by accident.

As far from Evie as you could wish to get was Brangwyn, still, in his mounting fifties, rumbling grandly on. Sir Frank Brangwyn R.A., grand old man of the grand old manner, was not a poster artist, but like so many non-poster artists before and since, having been persuaded to have a go, he got used to it.

He was born in 1865—the year Michael Faraday died. He died, ten years into the atomic age, in 1956. His work spans not just an era but a whole succession of eras. He saw the coming—and the going—of a score of fads and fancies. The Twenties was one of them.

Nurtured in the days when men were men and lithography was a man-size struggle with a two-hundredweight slab of limestone, Brangwyn's drawings had little about them that was prissy. His

Evie de Ropp (Cabaret), 1922 (France) *Aubrey Hammond*

EVIE
de
ROPP
AUBREY HAMMOND 1922
HARFORD. 34. R. DE CHABROL. PARIS.

subjects were the rough-hewn majesty of the foundry, the shove and sweat of the mason's yards; the docks and workshops, the building sites and the shipyards, the quarries and mines—these were the Brangwyn hunting ground.

Hunting was good. Like Fred Taylor and Norman Wilkinson, he was known as an 'industrial' artist—not the desk-bound 'industrial artist' of today, with his bow-tie and anglepoise, but an honest-to-God knock-'em-down-and-drag-'em-out genuine artist. He knew and understood—and liked—the man-size jobs that industry did.

In spite of the trade recession there was a lot of room for old men like Brangwyn. In the heavy industries, among the railway companies, in civil engineering, building and shipping there were important graphic jobs to be done. But big business was suspicious of the new-style 'abstract' and 'advanced' work of the new boys; they even wondered whether some of it was not just a huge hoax. They were also aware of big anti-advertising pressures that sought to bring poster advertising under stricter control. It was clearly safer to use proper artists than to risk being mixed up in a battle of aesthetics.

Brangwyn and the rest of the 'real artist' poster artists found themselves cited as the nucleus of a reform-in-advertising campaign. The newly-formed railway companies had lit on the bright idea of employing notable artists (Brangwyn among them) to show the public the landscape pleasures of the rail. In endless profusion these idyllic views appeared: by the reform faction they were enthusiastically hailed as 'examples of what *could* be done'. Why not employ real artists for all advertising? 'We need,' said one writer, 'a steady increase of original lithographs like Frank Brangwyn's *Royal Border Bridge* . . . Posters in flat tints, designed by good craftsmen, are reproduced very well by the best commercial lithographers, but original lithographs from a master's hand have a magnificent power in broad decoration.' It was with

Zambrene c. 1924 (Britain) *Sir Frank Brangwyn RA*

42

critics like this in mind that the railway companies—and indeed most transport organisations—gobbled up Newbould, Wilkinson, Taylor and Brangwyn and Company with renewed appetite. Brangwyn at one stage ran the risk of going down in history as a bridge artist.

Reform-minded products like Stephenson's Furniture Cream and Zambrene Raincoats weighed in with Brangwyn. Gerald Spenser Pryse did one for Sunlight Soap. The reform movement, a direct descendant of the 1890s Society for the Checking of Abuses in Public Advertising, was at times an embarrassment to advertisers and artists alike.

In America, threatened with a surfeit of bridges, the Chicago North Shore and Milwaukee Railroad people attempted to fight their way out with the blandishments of female golf. But it was no good. The landscapes came crowding back.

Ever since Toulouse-Lautrec's painful effort for bicycle chains the problem has been present. How wise is it for the artist to become universal aunt to a poster hoarding? How far should he get involved at all? And if he does, can he exist apart from advertising, as an artist in his own right? There were many who feared that Millais had done for himself when, although reluctantly, he allowed the Pears people to use his 'Bubbles' as a poster. There have been other cases. Brangwyn seems to have survived his Zambrene; perhaps he was lucky that it was not an all-time smash hit, as 'Bubbles' was. The balance of recollection might have been tipped. Certainly his superb posters during the 1914–18 War, known and remembered by millions, must have served as a link between the 'fine art' of his murals for the Canadian House of Parliament and his rubberless raincoats.

A Royal Academician since 1919, he was knighted in 1941. In 1952 they made him the first living artist to be honoured with a

North Shore Line 1923 (USA) *Willard Frederic Elmes*

44

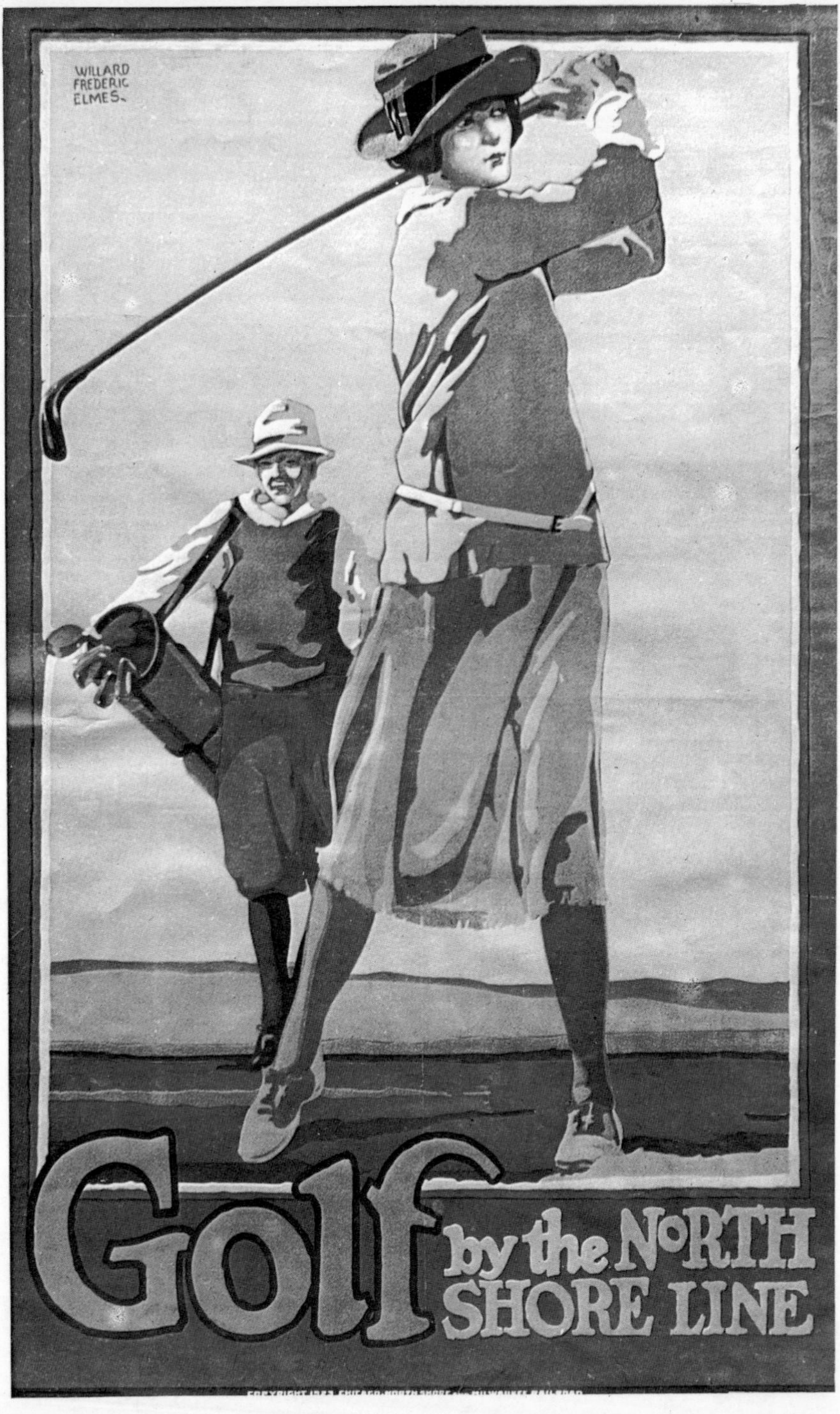
WILLARD FREDERIC ELMES
Golf by the NORTH SHORE LINE

retrospective exhibition at the Academy. The raincoat job was omitted.

While Britain's railways were playing safe with views of Shap Fell and Lincoln Cathedral by moonlight, France was cultivating the talents of a young man in his early twenties, late of Kharkov, Russia—name of Adolphe Mouron Cassandre.

When the Chemin de Fer du Nord linked with the Dutch and Belgian Railways in an international hook-up (Paris–Amsterdam daily, Pullman all the way) they called the service l'*Étoile du Nord.* They also called in Cassandre.

It would be an exaggeration to say that the train ran better, or that passengers enjoyed their trip more, on account of Cassandre. But it would be an exaggeration well worth risking. The *Étoile du Nord* design was among the first of the world's truly great posters. It had few of the statutory ingredients. Visual wit, a characteristic of the French poster of the 'twenties and 'thirties, is absent. So is the element of sex. So in fact is human interest of any kind. By standards of rule of thumb, this is scarcely a poster at all. But its visual impact, its almost hypnotic hold on the attention, its breathless directional drive to the distant point, its economy and its clarity make it all-compulsive.

It is a true poster; it owes nothing to the lithographic stone or to the canvas; it is not an adaptation of existing techniques and conventions—it speaks in an idiom of its own construction and it is an idiom that is instantly understood.

This was the beginning of something very big in France. In Britain it got off to a shaky start. Like the work of Kauffer, it was 'advanced'. Its arrival had been noted with impregnable unconcern; this sort of thing was all right for foreigners but for the work-a-day anglo-saxon world it was 'freakish and arbitrary'. In the very year that the *Étoile du Nord* appeared a London commentator observed that 'a comparison with the average French travel poster shows an

Etoile du Nord (International Pullman Service), 1927 (France)
Adolphe Mouron Cassandre

enormous superiority in England.' Shap Fell and Lincoln Cathedral stood their ground. The gap in outlook was to widen before it closed. In the late 'twenties and 'thirties the idiom of the continental poster was to gain currency with an enormous public. The Cassandre approach, vigorous, stimulating and direct, was to supersede the old pictorialism in all its forms. How far ahead of its time it was may be judged not only from the extraordinary contrast it made with its contemporaries, but from its complete acceptability to the eye of forty years on. It is an idiom that may well prove viable into the 'eighties and 'nineties.

Where other designers, by stealth or accident, had had posters thrust upon them, Cassandre was a poster man made-to-measure. He and Kauffer were new phenomena in professional standing, as well as style. They demolished for ever the idea of the 'artist who also does a poster now and again'. Poster design was no longer a sideshow. It was a life work.

But in Britain it was hard going. The tradition of 'Bubbles' and Brangwyn, R.A., was deeply engrained. It still is. If we compare the *Étoile du Nord* approach with *Hampton Court by Tram,* we see the strength of the resistance. On the one hand, a new and challenging impact—on the other, another dose of the old security, the Newbould-Taylor-Wilkinson mixture as before. (It must be said, by the way, that the Hampton Court design confuses the issue not only by the distraction of its Freudian overtones, but by the straightforward oddity of its *ménage à trois*. The woman in the background worries us; was she with them all the way on the tram too?)

Of the many examples of artists who had posters thrust upon them, perhaps Edward Wadsworth is the happiest. He was, at the same time an artist and an engineer—predicament enough for any man, it might be thought. But for Wadsworth there was the touch of

Underground Electric Railways Company c. 1926 (Britain) *Elijah Albert Cox*

48

HAMPTON COURT
BY TRAM

God in pawls and ratchets as well as in the earth and sky. (On one occasion he even addressed the Institute of Civil Engineers on *Aesthetic Aspects of Engineering*, but it is to be feared that he was readier to meet them half-way than they him.) His best-remembered work is in his near-surrealist still-lifes: anchors, buoys, fishing tackle; seafaring gear in a quayside clutter under an open sky—these were the Wadsworth paraphernalia and the raw material of his life's work.

As a younger man he had become engrossed with the dynamic effect of wartime naval camouflage (he had in fact served part of his time as a camouflage artist). The 'dazzle' technique of camouflage, introduced in the 1914–18 War, had inspired paintings by many artists, but Wadsworth's studies had an almost brutal brilliance. He exploited the interplay of patterns in the drydock setting, relating them to the camouflage patterns of the hulls of ships. He was an 'advanced' artist. Arnold Bennett made the point abundantly clear by denying it: 'I am not going to say that Mr Wadsworth is "advanced",' he said. But he went on to point out that in Wadsworth's studies of Black Country squalor—another of the artist's obsessions—'he has no use for that facile picturesqueness which any slick performer can paste over furnaces and slagheaps and grime. His courage may disconcert the timid,' he said, 'and a good thing too!' Like Brangwyn before him, Wadsworth was an 'industrial artist'—an 'ugly' painter, as some said.

When in 1923 the British Museum and the Board of Trade put on an exhibition of English Graphics in Zurich it was an 'ugly' Wadsworth—not a slagheap but the back end of a camouflaged battleship—that they used for the poster. Undaunted by its spelling error (the Swiss have always been confused about the spelling of Britisch) it shone out loud and clear from the Zurich hoardings. With its commanding pattern effect it was a poster to the manner born. Where the work of other artists had been mangled into posters, here was a case of 'fine art' out-postering the poster. Zurich was impressed to see the progress that the British poster

Wolfsberg Art Gallery (Exhibition of British Graphics), 1923 (Switzerland)
Edward Wadsworth

KUNSTSALON „WOLFSBERG"
AUSSTELLUNG
ENGLISCHE GRAPHIK
VERANSTALTET VOM BOARD OF TRADE
UND BRITHISH MUSEUM. LONDON. JUNI-AUGUST 1923
120 KÜNSTLER   2000 WERKE
GEÖFFNET 9-12 UND 2-6 UHR. SONNTAGS 10-12 UHR

„WOLFSBERG" ZÜRICH

had made. It is ironic—and perhaps symptomatic of how advanced he was—that the British were not to see his poster side until 1936, when London Transport latched on to him as an eye-catcher for the Imperial War Museum. Again with powerful impact, a Wadsworth camouflage piece became a poster—as 'contemporary' and up-to-the-minute as the middle 'thirties could wish. If it were republished today, half a century after its first emergence, it would be the same.

Catching the eye of the Londoner is only a microscopic part of the role of London Transport, but it is a job it has done with uncanny certainty since its very earliest days. Even before the London Passenger Transport Board of 1933 was formed, when it was still a loosely associated tangle of not-quite-separate interests, it was a focal point of design development. In recent times, freed from the normal commercial need to persuade, the success of its posters has been measured mostly by aesthetic criteria. More than a quarter of a century has passed since the system needed to sell itself; today, with only the most benign of avuncular encouragement, its posters merely preside at our comings and goings. Far from pressing travellers to increase the pressure, they sometimes serve as tranquillisers to the overpushed and overpacked.

But in the 'twenties the competitive element was still present. *Underground to anywhere—Quickest way, cheapest fare,* the early posters had said. *Kew Gardens by tram to Kew Bridge—* and there was even a coy one by C. R. W. Nevinson saying *Lovers to Lovers' Lanes by Motor Bus. Winter Sales are Best Reached by Underground,* said E. McKnight Kauffer in 1924. *The Roads are Never Up on the Underground,* said ex-Kitchener artist Alfred Leete. F. C. Herrick's listening girl, with her 2LO look and her genuine 1920s psychedelic background, is in similar vein. It was to become vestigial, but the tendency continued as though by Pavlovian reflex, far into the 'thirties.

Architect, midwife and mother-superior to London Transport— not only to its design policy, but to its whole structure—was Frank

Underground Electric Railways Company c. 1924 (Britain) *F. C. Herrick*

Pick. He started life as an articled clerk to a York solicitor and ended up as Vice-Chairman of the largest transport undertaking the world has ever known.

Pick was an inverted Edward Wadsworth; he was, at one and the same time, neither artist nor engineer. But he was the most sensitive non-artist and the most practical non-engineer of the twentieth century. 'All the elements of design,' he said, '—function, form and economy—make up an organic whole . . . for the designer in industry, the ability to co-operate with others is essential . . . Designers should be properly organised; they should adjust themselves to mass production, machine technique, and economic and commercial necessities, and should be trained on this basis in the schools. Industrialists should receive some training in industrial design, should extend their research habit of mind into the design side of their business, and should give the artist full recognition as an expert technician.'

Under Pick's influence the whole character of London Transport evolved. Rolling stock, station and equipment design, ticket machines, tickets—there was scarcely an item of transportalia that did not show signs of his presence.

It was Pick, back in 1917, who commissioned Edward Johnston to design a standard typeface for use throughout the whole system. (The type was to form the basis of *Gill Sans,* the typeface produced by Johnston's pupil, Eric Gill.) It was Pick who set Charles Holden loose on the organisation's architecture—thus founding a school of transport architecture that was to spread throughout the world. It was Pick who was responsible for getting both Epstein and Henry Moore to carve sculptures for the new building at 55 Broadway. It was he who was responsible for launching the careers of scores of graphic designers; he was ahead of Derry and Toms by three or four years with Kauffer. The London Transport list of poster artists reads like a graphic *Almanach de Gotha.* Dowd *(Ride*

London General Omnibus Company c. 1926 (Britain) *J. Dowd*

54

J.H. DOWD

RIDE GENERAL AND RIDE WELL

General and Ride well) was one of the early ones. Epstein (*Epping Forest,* 1934) was a bit later.

'He gave the public,' somebody said, 'not what he conceived that it wanted, but what it unquestionably needed—a visual education. There are only two ways with public taste: you must either lead or follow it. In a matter which was to him of such importance Pick was never content to follow.'

If London Transport did not sell itself to Londoners, it certainly sold them London. When it had run the gamut of Kew Gardens and Lovers' Lanes it started on the butterflies in the Natural History Museum, waterfowl on the park lakes, and the Elgin Marbles. It even sold the seasons of the year. Dora Batty's autumn and summer pieces are typical, not only of the 'twenties, but of an apparently inexhaustible public-relations effort—in London, for London, and about London.

These smaller posters, designed for close-quarters viewing, appeared as part of an occasional series for the glass dividers at tube-train carriage doorways. They are vintage Batty. Perhaps no other posters convey so vividly the prissy conventions of the Female Twenties; shaven and shorn, petalled and powdered, this is the ambiguous girl-boy image of emancipation.

If the fashion resurrectionists of the 'sixties have made us over-familiar with the image, we may need to remind ourselves that this was all of forty years ago. Hitler had just published volume two of *Mein Kampf,* Lindbergh had recently flown the Atlantic and from January 1st there had been a brand-new thing to replace the British Broadcasting Company—a corporation, as they called it. The first talking picture had just come out. Professor Alexander Fleming still had another year to go before he was to notice a circle of isolation around certain bacteria in a culture plate on an open window-sill in Praed Street.

In Praed Street itself the sound and smell of traffic was increasing daily. The time was fast approaching when Fleming was to keep the laboratory window permanently closed. With its sights fixed firmly on the target of the £100 motor car, the industry had

Underground Electric Railways Company 1927 (Britain) *Dora Batty*

been steadily improving its productivity. By 1926 the £100 car was a reality. By 1928 it was common. But the full range for family four-seater cars went right the way up to £900 and more. (The old-age pension, by way of contrast, was ten shillings a week.) It was clear that with the long-standing trade recession still no nearer improvement the chief market for motor cars was among the middle class. In the face of all discouragement (mechanical and financial) the middle class became motorborne as soon as it could. Mechanical hazards were many; discomfort and danger were part of the deal. All over Europe, almost all over the world, the intending motorist was plied with press and poster reassurance.

Of the Fiat 509, held aloft here by an earnest industrial centaur, *The Autocar* said 'It can be driven all out, all day, without tuning at all . . .' Assurances from all sides, whether from advertisers, road-test journalists or owners, had the knack of raising more doubts than they allayed. The poster (with its ambiguous man/ horse image of ancient Greece) is in the idiom of turn-of-the-century Industrial Mythology. It may be nonsense but it is strong nonsense, simple, positive and direct. It has the polyglot advantage of wordlessness. With huge potential markets outside Italy its universal validity gives it a big lead. But it goes no further than panache and prestige—and that, with a cone clutch and a crash gearbox, may not be quite enough.

It is the industry's own advertising that throws the strongest light on the state of the art at the time; between the lines the truth shines bright: 'A biting east wind, a long steep slope into the teeth of a gale—and driving rain to search every corner of hood and side curtains—these have no terrors for the occupants of a Sunbeam touring car . . .' 'The hydraulically operated four-wheel brakes on the new Studebaker make SKIDDING IMPOSSIBLE . . .' 'When you are stuck in the middle of a column of cars, moving along a hundred yards at a time, you value an engine that can keep on

Fiat 1925 (Italy) *Codognato*

FIAT 509

quietly ticking over. It is so ignominious to hold everyone up whilst you start up your "stalled" motor.' The copywriting of the day was a fine mixture of naivety and brutality. We notice the apology of the quotation marks on the word *stalled*. A new word.

'Twinbar spring bumpers absorb all bumps and shocks from collisions and preserve the new appearance of your car. Fit one in front and one at the rear.' 'At last a petrol filter which cannot possibly choke . . .' 'Two hours work on the motor leaves no grimy traces after two minutes work on your hands with Glitto . . .' 'Brasso cleans celluloid . . .' We are still in the days when a special all-weather motor oil, marketed under the name of *Zero Huile de Luxe,* is offered by Price's Patent Candle Company.

We are also still in the days when balloon tyres are a novelty. The Dunlop poster leaves as little doubt about their advantages as it does about the state of the roads. Neither point is really an exaggeration. With solid tyres still widespread and roads still in the 1890s, the balloon tyre was a luxury that everyone needed. But even the manufacturers sounded a note of caution; a handbook says: 'No driver running on pneumatics would take a big patch of newly-laid chippings at high speed without expecting a burst; on solids equal care is necessary, for high speeds over unrolled stones will destroy any tyre.'

Advertisers were still able to refer to each other's products—if not by name, then generically: 'Balloon tyres, with their extreme flexibility, large air capacity, and low pressure, give excellent results—up to a point. The point where they become the reverse of comfortable is when travelling moderately fast over a bad or wavy road. At that moment, balloon tyres . . . commence a galloping motion, which, in the case of cars not fitted with double action shock absorbers, quickly coincides with the action of the springs, and the result is a distressing fore and aft motion—a combination of galloping, pitching, rolling and sideswaying. There is only one

Dunlop 1925 (Germany) *Hinklein*

real remedy for this . . . To get the fullest possible benefit from balloon tyres . . . the suspension system of the car must be controlled by *shock absorbers*. . . .'

The business of keeping the car in continuous and controlled contact with the road was a big worry. The hazards of the elements from top and sides were equalled by those of unknown dangers beneath. As well as skidding, there was wheel wobble. Whether you had hard tyres or low- or high-pressure pneumatics, alarming vibrations were likely to break out. A passenger-correspondent in a motoring magazine reported, 'I was much struck by the fact that at critical speeds the front axle began to bounce up and down. The driver pushed the car up to 65, at which speed the steering wheel oscillated at about 40 times per second over something not far short of half a circle. Somewhere between 65 and 70—of the figure I cannot speak with exactitude, since the whole instrument board had become blurred—the driver crammed on the brakes and sat back literally gasping for breath.'

One advertiser, in a compendious piece of shock-absorber copywriting, said, 'Stop that bumping, bouncing, swaying, pitching, skidding, rattling, dithering.'

The thing was still very much in its infancy. But you could buy a motor car for £10 down, and people did.

The Bisto kids did not. Will Owen originated the drawing, but the originals of the kids themselves were real—the product of real poverty in times that were not quite gone. Their prototypes had been the scavenger-kids that Mayhew interviewed in Victorian London; their immediate forebears were the only slightly less wretched ones of Stepney and the Gorbals. But hallowed by time and by the goodwill of generations of British housewives, the Bisto kids have shed the Mayhew image. In the 'twenties, with unemployment permanently around the 1½-million mark, poverty was a reality and hunger only just below the surface. The smell of Bisto (which throughout the kids' existence has accounted for their beatific expressions) was the central theme of all their public

Bisto 1927 (Britain)*Will Owen*

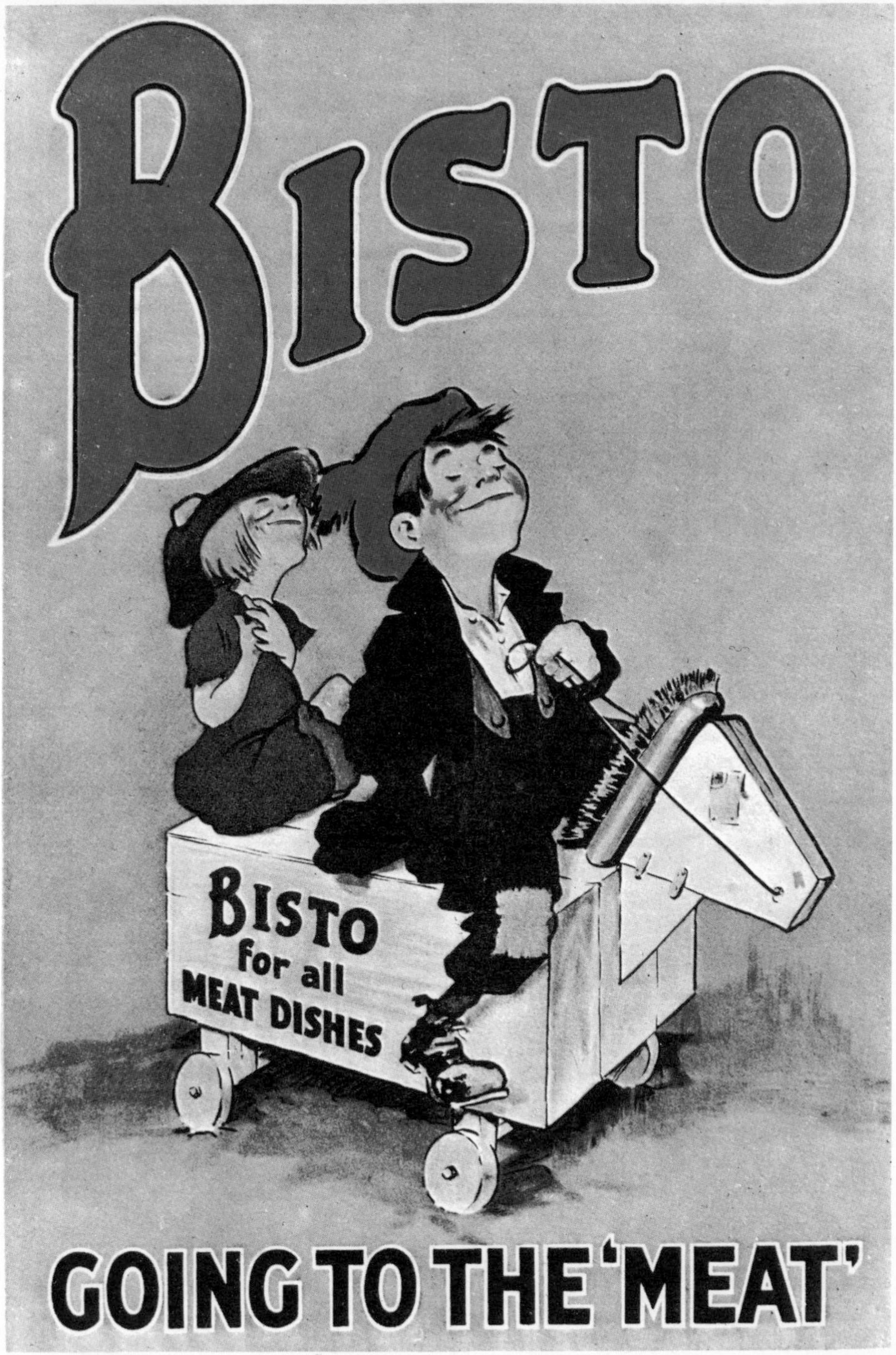
BISTO
BISTO
for all
MEAT DISHES
GOING TO THE 'MEAT'

appearances. It may well be that for Will Owen himself they expressed a joke that was only just a joke; their wide acceptance may suggest a folk-awareness shared by everyone. With the passing of the years and the coming of the welfare state the rags and patches of the pair have progressively disappeared; only their hugely appreciative sniffs of the product remain. For all its muddled undertones, the image still evokes nostalgia; among hundreds of thousands of survivors, this—rather than boop-a-doop—is the preferred version of the 'twenties.

The American 'twenties started with simple prohibition, moved on to bootlegging, gunrunning, hijacking, machine-gun gang-warfare and the world's record statistics for murder, armed robbery, burglary and graft. Working from just outside the 3-mile limit, a small fleet of foreign ships served an undercover distribution network; the entire country was crisscrossed with supply lines and outlets. Drink became everybody's big problem. In one year alone the Law seized 20 million gallons of alcoholic beverages and arrested nearly 80,000 people. Prohibition did not work.

There were big labour troubles. Wages had gone skyhigh during the war; unions refused to let them come down again. There were strikes. Europe had borrowed 10,000 million dollars to pay for the war; the money had not been returned. The economy did not work. After a decade of mounting difficulty, on 29 October 1929 the Stock Market crashed. Foreign trade petered out, factories closed, unemployment figures soared.

In the meantime, as in the Tivoli Gardens and Lyons Popular Café, they had danced. In the new emancipated syncopated world, where only a few years before dancing had been the prerogative of the evening-wrap set, now everybody could have a go. It worked. Helping to make it work, with their million-dollar clothes for men, were Hart Schaffner and Marx.

Their poster conveys the mood. Sparked off by the rage for rag-

Hart Schaffner and Marx c. 1923 (USA) *Anonymous*

64

time and jazz that had moved up from the south, a new kind of dancing had emerged; suddenly the worn-out polkas and waltzes and the tired imitations of Europe collapsed; suddenly everything was Thoroughly Modern. It stayed that way throughout the 'twenties.

In Germany there was no dancing. There was economic disaster and political and social unrest to the point almost of revolution. Inflation unparalleled in history was to sweep the country to chaos. It became severe in 1922, when the value of the mark dropped from 162 to the American dollar to 7,000. In 1923 it fell to 160,000; then to 242 *million*. On 20 November 1923, it took 4,200 *million million* marks to buy one American dollar. The price of a single copy of a newspaper was 200,000 million marks. Barter took over. Savings vanished.

Amid chaos on this scale there were few who retained the even balance of ordinary life. The few who applied themselves to creative matters were a tiny minority. One of them was Walter Gropius.

Architect, visionary, designer and strictly practical man, Gropius shines from the 'twenties like a light in almost total darkness. In the turmoil of post-war Germany he dedicated himself to one single objective—the bridging of the gulf between the designer and industry. In 1911 he had put up a remarkable new factory building that had placed him instantly at the head of the *avant-garde* in Europe. Not only as a designer but as an inspiration to the teams of creative people he gathered round him, his influence was to spread throughout the world. His *Bauhaus* art school/workshop/ architectural study-centre was a seedbed of design revolution. From it there stemmed new concepts of art in industry, new approaches to design in all its aspects—including the poster. The poster for the Advertising Exhibition, held in Berlin in 1929, is a link in a design chain that remains unbroken today.

Newcomers to the European poster field were the oil companies.

Advertising Exhibition 1929 (Germany) *Bernhard Rosen*

REKLAME
SCHAU
1929·BERLIN·10.AUG.-8.SEPT.

Still closely under the wing of poster tradition, still unresolved, both in their search for a design image and a viable structure of distribution, they trailed, can in hand, after the motorist. As they observed the bouncing up and down of his front axle they offered him higher speeds, more thrills, at less cost.

Jean d'Ylen's Shell poster is symptomatic. Published originally in Paris by the French section of the company, and adapted for English-speaking use, the can-carrying horse is a typical d'Ylen concept. With the petrol pump still only a novelty the product image of the early 'twenties centred strongly on the 2-gallon sealed can. In pre-war days the motorist had bought his petrol from ironmongers, village smithies, cycle agents, coaching stations, inns and even chemists' shops, as best he could. Only gradually did garages move into the petrol-selling business. The can was a great step forward, not only for the company for brand identification but to the motorist as a reserve supply to carry on the running board and a handy thing to walk to the nearest garage with when you ran out.

D'Ylen specialised in leaping figures on black backgrounds. Port wine, cigarettes, braces, champagne or paint—whatever it was the well-known formula saved the day. When Shell, like the other oil companies, came up with petrol pumps around 1924/5 they got him to abandon the flying figure for a four-square ground-based petrol pump. It somehow did not quite come off. Not least of the poster designer's problems is the fineness of the balance between a clearly recognisable style and clearly recognisable repetition.

As the 'twenties wained, Shell was within only a few years of the glorious days of Jack Beddington—art director and promotional *deus ex machina* of the petrochemical 'thirties. It was he who father-in-lawed the golden age, not only of *Crikey that's*

Shell 1923 (Britain) *Jean d'Ylen*

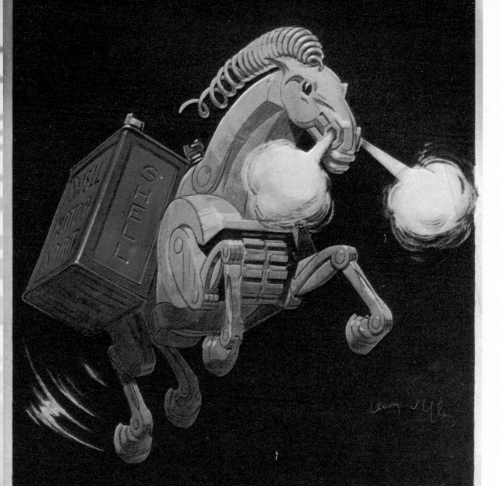

SHELL
FOR THE UTMOST
HORSE POWER

Shell, that was, but the endlessly successful theme, *You can be sure of Shell.* It was on boards on the backs of the trucks that carried the 2-gallon cans—and eventually, when pumps came in, the heavyweight tanks of spirit—that Beddington's team of artists had their famous heyday. With Frank Pick, Beddington ranks as associate architect of Britain's design renaissance. Across the boards of his trucks there passed the greatest names in the world of graphics. It is ironic that the best-remembered image of all— the double-headed *Crikey* series, in which a variety of characters are shown simultaneously watching the coming and going of a fast car—should have been anonymous. It was suggested to an artist in 1932 by 'an ordinary member of the public'.

Anonymous too is the winking lad with the choc-full chocolate bar. A pity, because he was 20 or 30 years ahead of his time. But then that is the thing about the 'twenties. They were.

Nestlé c. 1928 (Britain) *Anonymous*

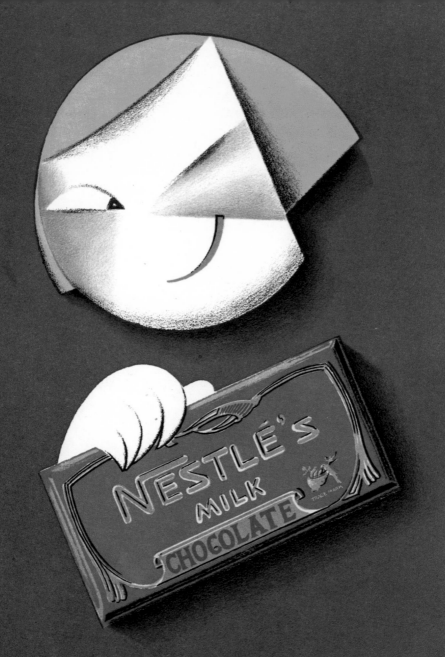

CHOC-FULL OF GOODNESS !

Acknowledgements

Among the many organizations and individuals who have helped in the preparation of this book the author and publishers would like especially to thank the staff of the Print Room of the Victoria and Albert Museum, and also London Transport for permission to feature the F. C. Herrick poster on the dust jacket.